Let Freedom Ring

The Mexican War, 1846–1848

by Susan E. Haberle

Consultant:
Charles M. Robinson, History Instructor
South Texas Community College
McAllen, Texas
Author of *The Men Who Wear the Star:
The Story of the Texas Rangers*

Bridgestone Books
an imprint of Capstone Press
Mankato, Minnesota

Bridgestone Books are published by Capstone Press
151 Good Counsel Drive, P.O. Box 669, Mankato, Minnesota 56002
http://www.capstone-press.com

Library of Congress Cataloging-in-Publication Data
Haberle, Susan E.
    The Mexican War, 1846–1848/by Susan E. Haberle.
        p. cm. — (Let freedom ring)
    Summary: Examines the causes and effects of the Mexican War and its
importance in the westward expansion of the United States.
    Includes bibliographical references and index.
    ISBN 0-7368-1558-9 (hardcover)
    1. Mexican War, 1846–1848—Juvenile literature. [1. Mexican War,
1846–1848.] I. Title. II. Series.
E404 .H33 2003
973.6'2—dc21   2002012001

Editorial Credits
Charles Pederson, editor; Kia Adams, series designer; Juliette Peters, book
designer; Kelly Garvin, photo researcher; Karen Risch, product planning editor

Photo Credits
California State Library, 37
Corbis, cover (inset), 17; Bettman, cover (main), 5, 11
Hulton Archive by Getty Images, 25, 35, 41
Illinois State Military Museum, 15
Library of Congress, cover (main), 19, 21, 27, 31
North Wind Picture Archives, 6, 7, 9, 29
Stock Montage, Inc., 22, 32, 43
Texas State Library & Archives Commission, 13, 42

1   2   3   4   5   6   0 8   0 7   0 6   0 5   0 4   0 3

Table of Contents

Chapter One

Before the War

The Mexican War (1846–1848) often gets little historical attention. Many people consider it less important than the earlier Revolutionary War (1775–1783). The Civil War (1861–1865) later overshadowed it. Unlike these other wars, the Mexican War involved only a small part of the United States.

The main cause of the Mexican War was a desire for land. In the early 1800s, the United States grew rapidly. In 1803, U.S. President Thomas Jefferson bought an area of land owned by France called the Louisiana Territory. This purchase spread the borders of the United States past the Mississippi River to the Rocky Mountains and from the Gulf of Mexico to Canada.

By the mid-1800s, the U.S. government wanted even more land, including the areas of present-day Texas, New Mexico, and California.

A U.S. representative formally receives the Louisiana Territory from a French official. The 1803 purchase nearly doubled the size of the United States.

Ulysses Grant and the War

Ulysses S. Grant was a lieutenant during the Mexican War. He later commanded the entire U.S. Army during the Civil War. In a book about his life, Grant wrote that the Mexican War was "one of the most unjust [wars] ever waged by a stronger [nation] against a weaker nation."

Mexico claimed these areas and did not want to lose them. Another cause of the war was the belief that God wanted the United States to control North America from the Atlantic Ocean to the Pacific Ocean. The belief was called manifest destiny. Many people believed in it. They did not care if Mexico or American Indians already claimed the land.

Mexican leaders also helped cause the war. Some of them hoped war would make the Mexican people forget the dishonesty of the government leaders. They wanted people to think about war instead of problems in Mexico.

Mexican Independence

Spain had a long history of ruling Mexico, which was called New Spain. In 1521, Spanish soldier Hernando Cortes defeated the Aztec people in Mexico, leading to hundreds of years of Spanish rule in the Americas. The Aztecs had to follow Spanish customs. Many became Roman Catholic, the main religion of Spanish leaders in Mexico. Some Mexicans became unhappy with Spanish rule because many of the leaders were dishonest.

On September 16, 1810, a Catholic priest named Miguel Hidalgo led a group of fighters to the capital, Mexico City. There, the Spanish-born leaders stopped the group. Hidalgo escaped to northern Mexico, where he was captured and killed. The Mexicans continued to fight for 11 years.

Miguel Hidalgo was a Spanish-born priest who led Mexican fighters in an attempt to take over the Mexican government. Mexican leaders stopped them and killed Hidalgo.

In 1821, under the rule of General Agustin Iturbide, Mexico finally won its independence from Spain. Two years later, Iturbide was thrown out. In 1824, the Republic of Mexico was created.

U.S. Settlers in Texas

While Mexico fought for independence in the early 1800s, U.S. settlers began moving into Mexican territory. Mexico was weak from its struggles with Spain and could not stop the settlers. U.S. Presidents John Quincy Adams and Andrew Jackson offered to buy Texas, but Mexico refused to sell it.

In 1821, U.S. citizen Stephen Austin made an offer to Mexico. He wanted Mexico to allow U.S. settlers to live in Texas. In return, the settlers promised to become Mexican citizens, join the Catholic faith, and obey Mexican laws. The Mexican government accepted Austin's offer.

Early U.S. settlers wanted to keep their promises, but the Mexican government provided little help. Because of this lack of help, many settlers kept their own customs and religion. When Mexico outlawed slavery, the settlers kept slaves anyway.

By 1834, more than 30,000 settlers from the United States lived in Texas. Only 7,500 Mexican-born people lived there. General Manuel Mier y Teran warned the Mexican government to help the settlers, but the government did not listen. Instead, it sent Mexican troops to Texas to force the settlers to obey. The troops failed. Their failure made it easier for later U.S. settlers to fight Mexico. Many of these later settlers never planned to cooperate with Mexico.

Mexican troops like these arrived in Texas to force the American settlers there to obey Mexican laws.

Chapter Two

Problems in Texas

Problems between Mexicans and American settlers in Texas began long before the start of the Mexican War. In 1834, General Antonio Lopez de Santa Anna became president of Mexico. He ruled with complete power as the country's dictator. Several Mexican states refused to obey Santa Anna. He took revenge. For three days, his soldiers robbed and killed the people in the Mexican city of Zacatecas. He wanted to show what happened to people who disobeyed him.

In 1835, Santa Anna sent Mexican troops to a river in Mexico called the Rio Grande. He planned to make the Texans obey him. He believed the sight of the Mexican army would scare the Texans into following his orders.

The sight of the troops angered the settlers. The

General Santa Anna was a long-time ruler of Mexico.
He ruled with complete power as a dictator.

Texans organized a group of civilian fighters to resist the Mexican army. General Sam Houston led this militia. Houston was a former soldier, congressman, and governor of Tennessee. Several hundred men joined his militia. In 1835, the militia took over the Texas towns of Gonzales and San Antonio.

The Battles of the Alamo and Goliad

Several battles were fought before the Mexican War officially started. The most famous was the Battle of the Alamo in 1836. The Alamo was a group of Spanish religious buildings in San Antonio. Mexican troops marched to San Antonio and attacked the Texas militia. The Mexicans greatly outnumbered the Texans. Only 189 Texas soldiers faced about 1,500 well-armed Mexican troops.

The surprised Texans quickly moved into the Alamo to protect themselves. The Texas leader, Colonel James Travis, asked for help. He wanted the militia at the nearby town of Goliad to send more troops and weapons. Nothing ever arrived. The Alamo defenders forced back the attacking Mexican soldiers. On their third try, the Mexicans broke through the walls of the Alamo. In a short battle, they killed all the Texans. The Alamo once again belonged to Mexico.

Santa Anna ordered his troops to burn the Texans' dead bodies.

When Houston learned about events at the Alamo, he ordered troops at Goliad to retreat. The Mexicans caught the retreating soldiers, who surrendered. Santa Anna ordered his soldiers to shoot the Texans. They killed more than 400 men.

In 1836, Mexican soldiers attacked the Texans defending the Alamo. The Mexicans captured and killed all the Texans inside the building.

The Battle of San Jacinto

The killings at the Alamo and Goliad angered Texans and U.S. citizens. Houston reorganized his army. In April 1836, he attacked the Mexican forces at the San Jacinto River in southeast Texas. Houston's army surprised the Mexicans during their afternoon rest, called a siesta. While attacking, Houston's army shouted, "Remember the Alamo!"

About 20 minutes later, the Mexicans surrendered. The Texas soldiers killed 600 Mexicans and wounded 200. They captured 730 men. One of them was Santa Anna, who agreed to remove his troops south of the Rio Grande. Houston allowed him to live and return to Mexico.

The Annexation of Texas

On March 2, 1836, Texas declared itself independent from Mexico. Sam Houston was chosen as the first president of the new Republic of Texas. But the Mexicans did not accept the independence of Texas. They still considered Texas part of Mexico. They thought of the Texans as criminals who must be chased from Texas.

Santa Anna's Leg

In December 1838, Santa Anna led a battle against French forces on the Mexican coast. His leg was wounded, and part of it had to be cut off. He had the amputated part buried.

In September 1842, Santa Anna wanted to remind the Mexican people of his heroism in battle. He decided to dig up and rebury his leg. A newspaper in Boston, Massachusetts, wrote: "Yesterday was buried, with great pomp and solemnity, in the [Mexico City] cemetery of St. Paul, the foot which his excellency, president Santa Anna, lost in the action of the 5th of December, 1838 . . ."

Santa Anna had a monument put up to mark the spot where his leg was reburied. He later used two wooden legs. During a battle in the Mexican War, U.S. soldiers captured one of Santa Anna's wooden legs, shown here.

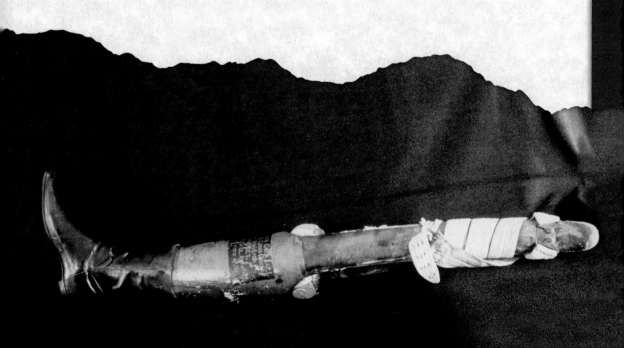

Many Texans wanted the U.S. Congress to make Texas a state, or annex it. Some Texans wanted the benefits of U.S. citizenship. Some Texans worried about further Mexican attacks. Many Texans wanted the U.S. Army to protect Texas if it became a state and Mexico attacked.

Opposing Views

The issue of slavery in Texas divided U.S. citizens. People living in the southern United States wanted another state where slavery was legal. People in northern states were against slavery and did not want another slave state. Both sides worried about losing political power if the other side won the slavery argument.

Mirabeau Lamar became president of Texas after Sam Houston left office. Houston had strongly supported annexation. Lamar was against it. He wanted Texas to expand west into New Mexico and California, which were part of Mexico. In 1841, Lamar sent wagons to open a trade route to Santa Fe, New Mexico. Mexican troops also traveled to Santa Fe. They captured the Texans and marched them to Mexico City, where they were put in prison.

Mexican leaders disagreed about war with the United States. Some leaders wanted a war if the United States annexed Texas. Mexican President Jose Joaquin Herrera was against war. He did not think Mexico had enough money to pay its soldiers. Also, he saw the United States had more people, better weapons, and a more powerful navy. Because Herrera was against the war, Mexican generals removed him as president.

Mirabeau Lamar was the second president of Texas, following Sam Houston. Lamar wanted to extend Texas lands west into New Mexico and California.

Chapter Three

War

The annexation of Texas was an issue in the U.S. presidential election of 1844. One candidate, Henry Clay, was against annexation. Another candidate, James Polk, was in favor of it. Polk won the election.

In July 1845, Texas citizens voted to have Texas join the United States. The Mexicans were angry about the vote and ended relations with the United States. Polk sent U.S. troops to Texas to prepare for a Mexican attack.

Several issues divided the United States and Mexico. They disagreed about Texas becoming a state. Mexico claimed Texas as Mexican territory. The two countries also disagreed on the border between Mexico and Texas. Texans believed the border should be the Rio Grande. The Mexicans believed the border should be the Nueces River. Texas and

Many Americans closely followed the news of war between Mexico and the United States.

Mexico claimed the land between the rivers. Mexico and the United States disagreed about who should control New Mexico and California.

In 1845, Polk sent John Slidell to Mexico to offer a deal. The United States would pay Mexico $5 million for New Mexico and $25 million for California. In return, Mexico would recognize the Rio Grande as the Texas-Mexico boundary. The offer angered Mexican leaders, who did not plan to give up any land. When Mexican leaders refused even to meet Slidell, U.S. officials felt insulted.

The First Shots

After learning of the Mexicans' actions, Polk sent General Zachary Taylor and a group of soldiers to Corpus Christi. This Texas town is located near the Nueces River. In January 1846, Taylor crossed the Nueces and built a fort on land that Mexico claimed. He aimed his cannons toward the Mexican town of Matamoros. His troops blocked the mouth of the Rio Grande. This blockade prevented supplies from reaching the Mexican army.

Mexican General Mariano Arista sent troops across the Rio Grande near Taylor's camp. Arista hoped the sight of his troops would convince the U.S. Army to retreat. Taylor had waited for this move. It provided him with an excuse to act.

On April 26, 1846, U.S. soldiers on patrol fought a group of Mexican troops. The Mexicans took the U.S. soldiers prisoner and brought them to Matamoros. Taylor reported that "American blood was shed on American soil."

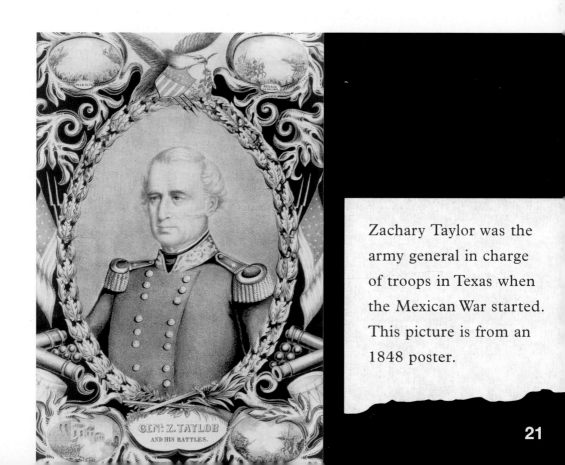

Zachary Taylor was the army general in charge of troops in Texas when the Mexican War started. This picture is from an 1848 poster.

On May 8, Taylor led his army at Palo Alto, where the first full-scale battle of the war was fought. The fighting was done mainly with cannons. The battle showed the strength of the U.S. Army and the advantage of using professional soldiers instead of volunteers. Nine American soldiers were killed. Another 43 were wounded. The Mexicans suffered about 200 killed and 125 wounded. The Mexican army withdrew overnight.

The next day, the two armies met at Resaca de la Palma, near Palo Alto. In the afternoon, the

The Battle of Palo Alto was the first full-scale battle of the Mexican War. It showed the strength of the U.S. Army.

U.S. troops began their attack. Later that day, the U.S. Army drove the Mexican soldiers from their position. In the battle, 33 U.S. soldiers were killed and 89 were wounded. Mexico claimed 154 men killed, 205 wounded, and 156 missing. Many of the missing probably drowned crossing the Rio Grande at night.

After these early U.S. victories, many more men joined the army. Some of these men were trained at the U.S. Military Academy at West Point, New York. Many academy graduates who fought in the Mexican War later became Civil War leaders. These leaders included Jefferson Davis, who became the South's president. Others were army generals Ulysses S. Grant, George Meade, James Longstreet, and Robert E. Lee. The battles at Palo Alto and Resaca de la Palma proved the value of using academy-trained army officers.

War Is Declared

On May 13, 1846, the U.S. Congress declared war against Mexico. U.S. citizens reacted to the war in various ways. Many people supported U.S. efforts to gain territory. They believed in manifest destiny. Some people believed the war would unite the country.

Other people were against the war. They thought the United States was misusing its power. A political party called the Whigs believed people in the southern states were using the war as an excuse to spread slavery. Some people thought the war would be too expensive for the United States. Congressman Abraham Lincoln tried to pass a law blaming the United States for the war. Writer Henry David Thoreau was jailed when he refused to pay taxes that would be used in support of the war.

Life in War

Most U.S. soldiers experienced a hard life in the Mexican War. Many soldiers were in their late teens or early 20s. Few had ever been away from home. They wanted glory and adventure. Instead, they faced long, hot marches, boredom, illness, injuries, and death.

Illness killed twice as many soldiers as enemy weapons did. Poor health habits spread measles, dysentery, and other diseases. Dysentery infects the intestines and causes serious or fatal diarrhea.

Doughboys

During the Mexican War, soldiers who rode on horseback called the foot soldiers "adobies." They used this word because the road dust that often covered the foot soldiers was the color of the mud-brick adobe buildings along the road. Soon, the name was changed to "dobies" and later to "doughboys." In the years after the Mexican War, many people called U.S. soldiers "doughboys."

Chapter Four

Fighting in Mexico

American leaders believed its army would have to conquer Mexico City before the war ended. Beginning in September 1846, many battles were fought for control of Mexico City.

One battle took place while the army marched into Mexico. The battle began in Monterrey, located in northern Mexico near the Rio Grande. Zachary Taylor's soldiers attacked two sides of the city at once. For three rainy days, Mexican soldiers fiercely fought U.S. soldiers. When U.S. soldiers nearly destroyed the Monterrey cathedral with cannon fire, the Mexicans surrendered. They did not want their church ruined.

By this time, Taylor's army had grown much larger with the arrival of new troops. Many of these men were volunteers from various states.

For three days, U.S. soldiers attacked the town of Monterrey. The Mexican defenders finally surrendered when the Americans threatened to use cannons to destroy the Monterrey cathedral.

They were not used to obeying orders the way regular soldiers were. Some volunteers burned Mexican houses and stole possessions. Taylor publicly blamed the volunteers. At first, he did nothing to punish them. Later, near the war's end, he began sending some of them home.

Buena Vista and Veracruz

Taylor and his troops moved farther into Mexico. In February 1847, they reached Buena Vista, 500 miles (805 kilometers) from Mexico City. At Buena Vista, they met troops under Santa Anna's command. The Mexican soldiers retreated after a day of bloody fighting. At least 500 Mexicans died, and about 750 U.S. soldiers were killed, wounded, or missing.

In March 1847, navy ships carried army General Winfield Scott and 14,000 soldiers to the seaside city of Veracruz, Mexico. Scott wanted to get there ahead of yellow fever season so his men would not get sick. Yellow fever caused a high fever, muscle pain, headaches, and vomiting. It killed many soldiers. Scott hoped to end the war before the disease became a problem for his troops.

The U.S. forces believed they needed to capture Veracruz before attacking Mexico City. After days of shelling by U.S. naval ships, the military commander of Veracruz surrendered to Scott.

Onward to Mexico City

Mexico's National Highway was an important route from Veracruz to Mexico City. It was better than many U.S. roads because it was paved. Still, it had few military defenses. After the Battle of Veracruz, Mexicans began to expect an attack on Mexico City.

General Winfield Scott and 14,000 U.S. soldiers landed at the Mexican town of Veracruz. After naval ships shelled the town for several days, the Mexican defenders surrendered.

The San Patricios

A large number of U.S. soldiers were Irish and German Roman Catholics. Santa Anna claimed the United States wanted to destroy the Catholic faith in Mexico. He encouraged Catholics in the U.S. Army to join the Mexicans in protecting the Catholic faith. About 200 men left the U.S. Army. The group's commander, John Riley, named them "Saint Patrick's Company." Mexicans called them the San Patricios.

During the Battle of Mexico City, 72 San Patricios surrendered. The U.S. Army held military trials and hanged 50 of the men. Some were not hanged because they were too young. Riley was not hanged, but he was whipped and had the letter "D" for "deserter" burned into his cheek.

By war's end, other men had joined the San Patricios. After the war, they continued serving in the Mexican Army. They patrolled border areas and later tried to help overturn the Mexican government. After the Mexican War, most San Patricios remained in Mexico because they did not have enough money to return to Ireland or Germany. They could not return to the United States because they had acted against it.

They blocked the highway and stored supplies along it. Santa Anna set up defenses at Cerro Gordo, a village located near steep hills on the highway.

In April 1847, U.S. troops surprised the Mexicans. They climbed the steep hills and attacked Cerro Gordo from several directions. The Americans used rope to pull supplies and heavy cannons up the hills. When the Mexican soldiers retreated, they left behind supplies Santa Anna had planned to use at Mexico City.

Hand-to-hand fighting took place at the Battle of Cerro Gordo. The U.S. troops surprised the Mexicans by attacking from several directions at one time.

After four months, Scott moved on to Mexico City. The city was heavily guarded except for a lake on the south end. The armies fought hard at the lake, but Mexican troops could not stop the U.S. soldiers.

Fighting stopped briefly as Mexico and the U.S. government discussed ending the war. Talks broke down as the two sides disagreed again on the U.S. and Mexican border. They disagreed about who should pay for war damages. The fighting continued.

The Halls of Montezuma

On September 10, 1847, one of the war's hardest-fought battles took place at a hill called Chapultepec. The hill was on the west side of Mexico City. Mexico's National Military Academy building sat on top of Chapultepec. The academy was

The last battle of the war was fought at Chapultepec, the Mexican military academy in Mexico City. The last six defenders fought to their deaths rather than surrender.

War in the West

Besides Texas, the United States wanted New Mexico and California. These Mexican lands offered good trade routes and seaports. Soon after the war began, Polk sent General Stephen Kearny's army to take over these areas. Kearny's army had 1,600 volunteers and 1,000 regular soldiers. The Americans peacefully took over Santa Fe and the rest of New Mexico.

In June 1846, U.S. Army Captain John Frémont led the Bear Flag Revolt in California. The fighters in the revolt were settlers who carried a flag with a picture of a grizzly bear on it. Kearny, Frémont, navy Admiral John Drake Sloat, and navy Commodore Robert Stockton conquered several California towns. On January 13, 1847, Frémont and the Mexican commander agreed to end the fighting in California.

called the Halls of Montezuma, after the one-time Aztec ruler Montezuma. It was a symbol of Mexican heritage and a national landmark.

Near the end of the fighting, the last six Mexican defenders fought to their death rather than surrender. One jumped from the academy walls. The six men became symbols of Mexican pride. The Battle of Chapultepec was the last battle of the war.

Chapter Five

The End of the War

In October 1847, Polk sent U.S. official Nicholas Trist to help General Winfield Scott arrange a treaty with Mexico. Scott's takeover of Mexico City had led to Santa Anna's downfall. Santa Anna had resigned and left in disgrace for the Caribbean island of Jamaica. Without Santa Anna, no one was left to meet with U.S. leaders. Trist and Scott waited for Mexico to select new leaders.

Manuel de la Peña y Peña became Mexico's temporary president. On February 2, 1848, Peña, Scott, and Trist signed a peace agreement in the town of Guadalupe Hidalgo. In the Treaty of Guadalupe Hidalgo, the United States paid Mexico $15 million for land. The money was supposed to help Mexico rebuild itself. By August, the U.S. troops had withdrawn from Mexico.

Winfield Scott, above, along with Nicholas Trist, met with Manuel de la Peña y Peña. The men signed an agreement to end the Mexican War.

Results for the United States

People in the United States disagreed about the Mexican War's outcome. Some wanted to take over all of Mexico. Other people thought it would be difficult to govern a country so different from the United States. Still other people did not like the idea of Mexicans marrying white Americans. Others wanted to allow Mexicans to keep their freedom.

The Treaty of Guadalupe Hidalgo increased the size of the United States by nearly one-third. It added California and New Mexico to U.S. territory. The area later was divided into the states of California, Nevada, Utah, and parts of Arizona, Wyoming, and Colorado. The Rio Grande became the official border of Texas.

The treaty also gave the United States lands rich in natural resources. In late January 1848, gold was found in California. The news did not reach the eastern United States until almost a year later. By

The California Gold Rush

After the Mexican War, California passed from the control of Mexico to the United States. In 1848, settlers discovered gold in California. Hearing of the discovery, many people traveled from the eastern United States to seek gold in the West.

In early 1848, only a few thousand people lived in California. By 1852, more than 250,000 people lived there. Many did not find any gold. Some unsuccessful gold seekers returned east. Others stayed and opened businesses, became farmers, or worked for mining companies.

the spring of 1849, thousands of U.S. citizens had rushed to California to look for gold. The gold rush contributed to U.S. westward expansion and an improved economy.

After the war, the United States controlled land from the Atlantic Ocean to the Pacific Ocean. The California ports made it easier to trade with countries around the Pacific Ocean. Trading with these countries was important in making the United States one of the world's richest countries.

The war was a military victory for the United States, but it upset the balance between slave and nonslave states. Texas joined the United States as a slave state. California and Nevada became nonslave states. This division between slave and nonslave states was one factor leading to the Civil War in 1861.

The Mexican War, 1848

BRITISH TERRITORY

Sutter's Fort
•San Francisco
• Monterey

• Los Angeles

Fort Leavenworth

• Santa Fe

UNITED
STATES

TEXAS

Rio Grande

Nueces River

MEXICO

• Corpus Christi

✳ Palo Alto
✳ Matamoros

Monterrey ✳
Buena Vista ✳

Gulf of
Mexico

PACIFIC
OCEAN

Guadalupe Hidalgo
•
Mexico City ✳
Cerro Gordo ✳   ✳ Veracruz

LEGEND

▨	U.S. Territory
▨	Mexican Territory
▨	Claimed by Mexico and United States
▨	British Territory
▨	U.S. Territory by Treaty, 1848
▨	Other Countries
⬆	Fort
•	Town
✳	Battle Site

The Mexican War resulted in the loss of many lives. More than 5,800 U.S. men were killed or wounded during the war. About 11,000 more died from disease. The war cost the United States about $75 million.

Results for Mexico

The war ruined Mexico. The exact number of Mexican soldiers who were killed or wounded is not known. Some estimates say it was as many as 14,700. Many Mexican cities and roads were damaged or destroyed. Mexico's economy was hurt. The country lost much of its territory, and its government was disrupted. This confused state later led to a civil war in Mexico.

The loss of the war to the United States angered many Mexicans. The war caused some Mexicans to dislike the United States for many years.

President Zachary Taylor

General Zachary Taylor's military victories at Palo Alto, Resaca de la Palma, Monterrey, and Buena Vista made him popular with many American voters. During the 1848 presidential election, his military reputation helped voters decide to elect him the 12th president of the United States. On July 4, 1850, he became ill. Five days later, he died. Taylor served as president for about 16 months of his four-year term.

TIMELINE

Hernando Cortes conquers the Aztec Empire.

February: The Battle of the Alamo begins in San Antonio, Texas.

March: Texas declares itself independent of Mexico.

March: The Alamo falls to Mexican troops.

1521   1821   1836   1844

Mexico gains its independence from Spain.

James Polk wins the U.S. presidential election.

Congress annexes Texas to
the United States.

February: Zachary
Taylor's forces win the
Battle of Buena Vista.

May: Congress declares
war on Mexico.

March: Mexican forces
at Veracruz surrender to
Winfield Scott's forces.

January: Gold is
discovered near Sutter's
Mill, sparking the
California gold rush.

August: Stephen
Kearny's army occupies
Santa Fe.

April: The Battle of
Cerro Gordo is fought.

1845   **1846**   **1847**   **1848**

February: The Treaty of
Guadalupe Hidalgo is signed,
ending the Mexican War.

September: U.S. forces attack
Chapultepec during the last
battle of the Mexican War.

September: Winfield Scott's
army occupies Mexico City.

Glossary

amputate (AM-pyuh-tate)—to cut off someone's arm, leg, or other body part, usually because the part is damaged

annexation (an-ek-SAY-shuhn)—the act of combining two territories into one

blockade (blok-ADE)—a closing off of an area to keep people or supplies from going in or out

dictator (DIK-tay-tur)—someone who has complete control of a country, often ruling it unjustly

dysentery (DISS-en-ter-ee)—a serious infection of the intestines that causes severe diarrhea

manifest destiny (MAN-uh-fest DESS-tuh-nee)—the belief that God gave white Americans the right to take over lands that belonged to other people

militia (muh-LISH-uh)—a group of citizens who are trained to fight but who only serve in time of emergency

natural resources (NACH-ur-uhl REE-sorss-uhz)—raw materials from nature, such as oil or minerals

siesta (see-ESS-tuh)—an afternoon period of rest, common in Spanish-speaking countries

treaty (TREE-tee)—a formal agreement between two or more groups of people or countries

yellow fever (YEL-loh FEE-vur)—a dangerous disease that mosquitoes carry and can pass to humans

For Further Reading

Boraas, Tracey. *Sam Houston: Soldier and Statesman.* Let Freedom Ring. Mankato, Minn.: Bridgestone Books, 2003.

Carey, Charles W. *The Mexican War: "Mr. Polk's War."* American War Series. Berkeley Heights, N.J.: Enslow Publishers, 2002.

Collier, Christopher. *The Cotton South and the Mexican War, 1835–1850.* Drama of American History. New York: Benchmark Books, 1998.

Garland, Sherry. *Voices of the Alamo.* New York: Scholastic Press, 2000.

Isaacs, Sally Senzell. *Life at the Alamo.* Picture the Past. Chicago: Heinemann, 2003.

Raabe, Emily. *The Mexican-American War.* Westward Ho! New York: PowerKids Press, 2003.

Thro, Ellen. *Growing and Dividing.* The Making of America. Austin, Texas: Raintree Steck-Vaughn, 2001.

Places of Interest

The Alamo
300 Alamo Plaza
P.O. Box 2599
San Antonio, TX 78299

The museum includes items that fighters used during the Battle of the Alamo.

The Bob Bullock Texas State History Museum
Corner of Martin Luther King Jr. Boulevard and North Congress Avenue
P.O. Box 12874
Austin, TX 78711

Visitors to the museum can find exhibits and information about Texas history.

Palo Alto Battlefield National Historic Site
1623 Central Boulevard
Suite 213
Brownsville, TX 78520-8326

The National Park Service preserves the site of the first major battle of the Mexican War.

Sam Houston Memorial Museum
1402 19th Street
P.O. Box 2057
Huntsville, TX 77341

The life and times of the great Texas leader are explored at this museum.

San Jacinto Battleground State Historic Site
3523 Battleground Road
LaPorte, TX 77571

A museum and monument are located on the grounds of the San Jacinto battlefield.

The Santa Fe Trail Center
Highway K-156
Rural Route 3
Larned, KS 67550

The Santa Fe Trail Center is located 2 miles (3 kilometers) west of Larned, Kansas, on Highway K-156. Indoor and outdoor exhibits tell about the history and importance of the Santa Fe Trail.

Internet Sites

Do you want to learn more about the Mexican War?
Visit the FACT HOUND at *http://www.facthound.com*

FACT HOUND can track down many sites to help you.
All the FACT HOUND sites are hand-selected
by Capstone Press editors. FACT HOUND will fetch the best,
most accurate information to answer your questions.

IT IS EASY! IT IS FUN!
1) Go to *http://www.facthound.com*
2) Type in: 0736815589
3) Click on "FETCH IT," and
   FACT HOUND will put you
   on the trail of several helpful links.

You can also search by subject or book title. So, relax
and let our pal FACT HOUND do the research for you!

Index